WOMAN OF GOD

60-DAY
DEVOTIONAL

WOMAN
of GOD

Devotions and Prayers
to Embrace God's Call and
Fulfill His Purpose

Candace Writes

ROCKRIDGE
PRESS

First Rockridge Press trade paperback edition 2022

Rockridge Press and the Rockridge Press logo are trademarks or registered trademarks of Callisto Media Inc. and/or its affiliates in the United States and other countries and may not be used without written permission.

For general information on our other products and services, please contact our Customer Care Department within the United States at (866) 744-2665, or outside the United States at (510) 253-0500.

Paperback ISBN: 978-1-63878-717-4 | eBook ISBN: 978-1-68539-947-4

Manufactured in the United States of America

Art Director: Helen Bruno
Interior and Cover Designer: Kristina Spencer
Art Producer: Maya Melenchuk
Editor: John Makowski
Production Manager: Lanore Coloprisco

Author photo courtesy of Emma Cheshire, We Dream Photography.
Illustrations © Olga Koelsch/Creative Market.

10 9 8 7 6 5 4 3 2 1 0